EDGE
BOOKS™

W9-BBC-463

Build It
Yourself

BUILD YOUR OWN
CAR, ROCKET,
AND OTHER THINGS THAT GO

BY TAMMY ENZ

CAPSTONE PRESS
a capstone imprint

Edge Books are published by Capstone Press,
151 Good Counsel Drive, P.O. Box 669, Mankato, Minnesota 56002.
www.capstonepub.com

Books published by Capstone Press are manufactured with paper
containing at least 10 percent post-consumer waste.

Library of Congress Cataloging-in-Publication Data
Enz, Tammy.
    Build your own car, rocket, and other things that go / by Tammy Enz.
    p. cm.—(Edge books. Build it yourself)
    Includes bibliographical references.
    ISBN 978-1-4296-5437-1 (library binding)
    ISBN 978-1-4296-6260-4 (paperback)
1. Transportation engineering—Juvenile literature. I. Title.
TA1149.E59 2011
629.04078—dc22   2010032204

Editorial Credits
Aaron Sautter, editor; Ted Williams, designer; Marcy Morin, project production;
    Eric Manske, production specialist

Photo Credits
All images from Capstone Press/Karon Dubke, except:

Shutterstock/CLM (spool), 6; DenisNata (tape measure), cover; eyed
    (washers), 22, 23; Feng Yu (rubber bands), 15, 20; Georgios Alexandris
    (toothpick), 26; Ljupco Smokovski (paper clip), 24, 25; M.E. Mulder (tape),
    8, 9, 10; Roman Sigaev (nail), 18, 19; STILLFX (clip), 9, 10

Design Elements/Backgrounds:
Shutterstock/ARENA Creative, Eky Studio, Nanka, romvo, Vector

Capstone Press would like to thank Isaac Morin for his help in producing the
projects in this book.

Printed in the United States of America in Stevens Point, Wisconsin.

062011   006228WZVMI

Table of Contents

4 Ready ... Set ... Build!

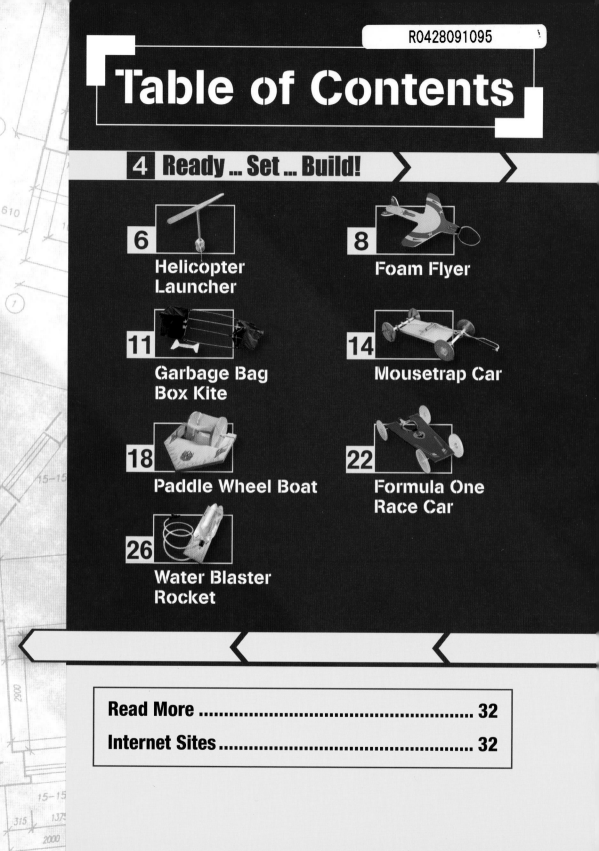

Do you love cars, airplanes, and other things that move? Then this book is for you! Inside you'll find some great ideas for building things that go.

Want to launch a homemade rocket into the air? How would you like to build your own mousetrap car? Just follow the simple instructions on the following pages. It won't take long, and you don't need to buy any special materials. You'll probably find everything you need around your house.

These projects are fun, but be careful when launching your creations. Safety is always the number-one rule. You don't want to get hurt or hurt someone else. And always be sure to ask an adult to help you with sharp tools. Now what are you waiting for? Go build something!

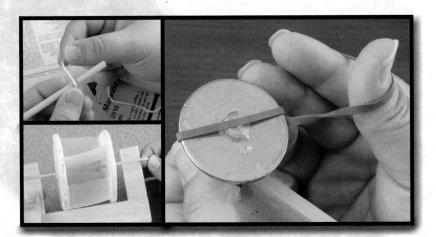

GATHER YOUR GEAR

Before you start building, take a few minutes to gather the tools listed below. Keep them organized in a toolbox so you can build your projects quickly.

MEASURING AND MARKING TOOLS

☐ pencil   ☐ ruler   ☐ tape measure

TIGHTENING AND LOOSENING TOOLS

☐ stapler   ☐ screwdrivers   ☐ hammer

☐ masking tape   ☐ electrical tape   ☐ hot glue gun

CUTTING AND SHAPING TOOLS

☐ drill   ☐ rasp   ☐ coping saw

☐ can openers   ☐ metal snips   ☐ scissors

☐ wire stripping tool   ☐ hand saw   ☐ pruning shears

☐ sandpaper   ☐ utility knife   ☐ wire snips

GRIPPING TOOLS

☐ needle-nose pliers   ☐ pliers

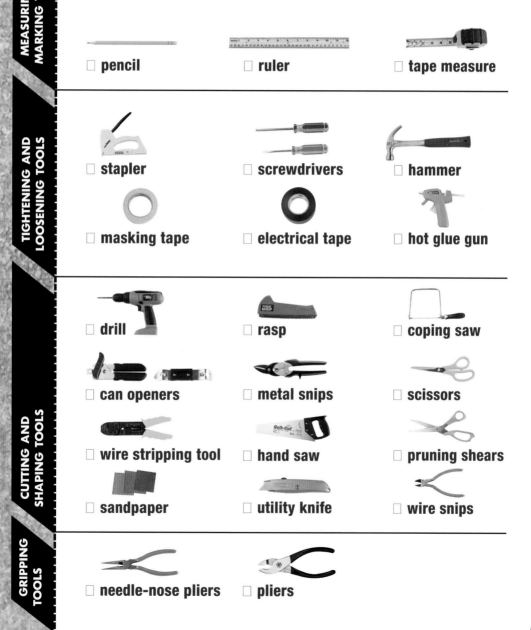

Helicopter Launcher

You'll have a blast launching this spinning helicopter into the air. Watch it sail high into the sky before it gracefully flutters to the ground.

MATERIALS

- wooden popsicle stick
- 1 wooden dowel,
  ³/₁₆ inch (.5 cm) thick by
  6 inches (15 cm) long
- gloves
- empty thread spool
- 2 feet (.6 m) of string
- epoxy glue
- microwave-safe dish

1 Ask an adult to microwave 2 cups (.5 l) of water in the dish until it begins to boil (about 6 minutes.) Remove the bowl with pot holders. Place the popsicle stick in the hot water for one minute.

2 Remove the stick from the water with a fork. Put on the gloves, then hold one end of the stick in each hand. Twist the stick ends in opposite directions as far as possible. Hold it like this until it cools. Repeat this step until the stick remains twisted when cool.

Apply the epoxy glue with a toothpick to attach one end of the dowel to the center of the stick.

Measure and mark one inch from the other end of the dowel. Hold the string on this mark and wrap it several times around the dowel.

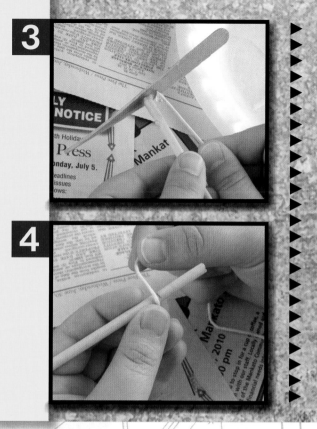

3

4

5

Place the end of the dowel into the center hole of the spool. Hold the spool in one hand, then quickly pull the string. The helicopter will spin and launch high into the air.

TIP This helicopter can be a little unpredictable. Be sure nobody is near you when launching it.

Foam Flyer

Ever dream of flying through the clouds in your own airplane? Now you can test your piloting skills with this high-soaring flyer. The sky is the limit!

 ## MATERIALS

- foam board, ⅛ inch (.3 cm) thick
- medium binder clip
- large rubber band
- tape
- paints or markers
- 8½ by 11-inch (22 by 28-cm) sheet of paper

1

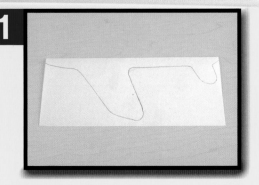

Fold the paper in half lengthwise. Draw one half of an airplane on the paper.

2

Use scissors to cut out the paper plane following the drawing from step 1. Unfold the paper, and then trace the outline of the plane onto the foam board.

3

Ask an adult to help you cut out the foam plane with a utility knife. Smooth out any rough edges with sandpaper.

4

Score two lines across the tail to make the tail flaps. Be sure not to cut all the way through the foam. Turn the plane over. Bend the flaps up and tape them at a 45-degree angle.

5

Use paints or markers to decorate the flyer any way you wish.

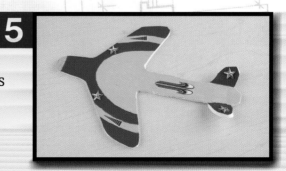

6

Place a rubber band inside the binder clip. Attach the clip to the nose of the plane.

Place the rubber band on the tip of your finger. Gently pull the plane back to stretch out the rubber band. Let go of the plane and watch it sail!

7

TIP Don't pull the flyer too far back when you launch it. The rubber band may pull the clip off and cause it to hit your finger.

Garbage Bag Box Kite

Few things are as fun as flying a kite on a windy day. Box kites are some of the coolest kites around. This box kite is easy to make and a lot of fun to fly.

✂ MATERIALS

- 4 dowels, ³/₁₆ inch (.5 cm) thick by 36 inches (91 cm) long
- Poster mounting putty
- 4 dowels, ³/₁₆ inch (.5 cm) thick by 12 inches (30 cm) long
- Black garbage bag
- 20 to 30 feet (6 to 9 m) of kite string

1

Lay two short dowels across each other at their centers. Tightly wrap the dowels together with electrical tape to form a cross piece. Repeat this step with the other short dowels to make a second cross piece.

⚠ *Keep Building!* ▶ 11

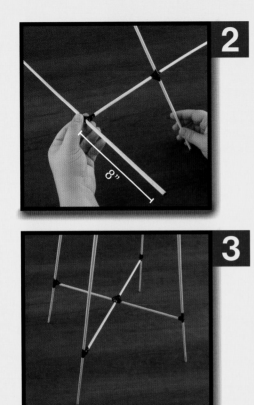

2

Measure and mark 8 inches (20 cm) from each end of each long dowel. Use putty to attach a tip of one cross piece to a long dowel at one of the marks. Tightly wrap this point with electrical tape.

3

Attach the other tips of the cross piece to the other long dowels as in step 2.

Attach the second cross piece at the marks on the other end of the long dowels. Adjust the joints as needed to make the kite square. Add extra tape to strengthen any loose joints.

4

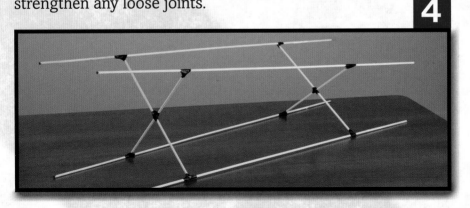

5 Cut a strip of garbage bag 8 inches (20 cm) wide. Wrap the strip around one end of the kite and tape it to the dowels. Repeat this step at the other end of the kite. Leave the center and ends of the kite open.

Tie the string to one joint where the short and long dowels are attached. Your kite is ready for its first flight!

6

TIP Take the kite out on a breezy day. With your back to the wind, lift the kite into the air. Gently pull the string up and down to get the kite to rise. Release more string as it rises higher.

Mousetrap Car

Mousetraps can have more uses than just catching mice. Put the power of a mousetrap to work to make this car run. Be careful not to snap your fingers!

✂ MATERIALS

- 1 mousetrap
- small rubber bands
- heavy string
- 4 eyehook screws, 1 ⅛ inches (2.9 cm) long
- 4 large washers, 2 inches (5 cm) wide
- 2 wooden dowels, ³/₁₆ inch (.5 cm) thick by 3 inches (7.6 cm) long

1

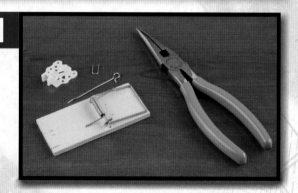

Use pliers to remove the metal parts of the mousetrap, but leave the spring and lever.

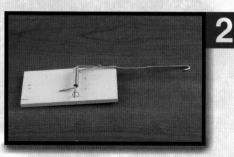

2

Remove the hooked end of the lever from the spring. Straighten out the wire, but leave the hook in the end. Position the lever so it points straight back behind the trap.

Ask an adult to help you drill four small holes about ¼ inch (.64 cm) from each corner of the mousetrap. Screw one eyehook into each hole. Be sure not to split the wood.

3

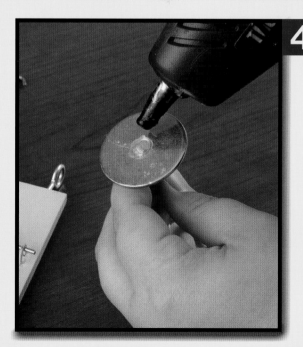

4

Place the end of one dowel into a washer. Ask an adult to help glue the washer in place with hot glue. Repeat this step with the second dowel.

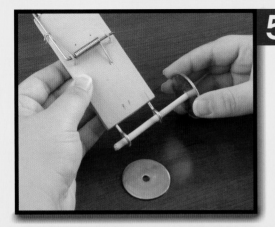

5

Slide the dowels through the eyehooks to form the car axles. Then repeat step 4 on the other ends of the dowels.

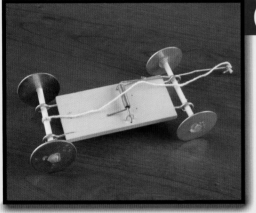

6

Cut a piece of string about 12 inches (30 cm) long. Tie one end to the hook on the lever. Tie the other end to the back axle. Use hot glue to hold the tied ends in place.

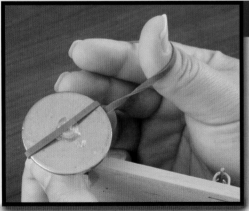

7

Wrap 2 or 3 rubber bands around each back wheel. The rubber bands will provide traction for the car.

Carefully lift the lever while winding the string counterclockwise onto the back axle.

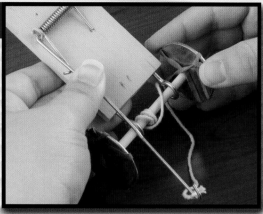

TIP

Mousetrap springs are very powerful. Be sure to hold the lever tightly while building and playing with this car.

When the string is wound tight, it's time to launch the car. Hold the lever in place and carefully set the car on the floor. Release the lever and watch your car take off!

Paddle Wheel Boat

Here's your chance to be the captain of your very own boat. You'll have tons of fun watching this little boat chug across the water.

✂ MATERIALS

- 1 soup can
- foam board, ⅛ inch (.3 cm) thick
- heavy rubber band
- 1 large nail
- 1 piece of balsa wood, 5 inches (13 cm) wide by 5 inches (13 cm) long by ¼ inch (.64 cm) thick
- 4 strips from a plastic milk jug, 1 inch (2.5 cm) wide by 2½ inches (6.4 cm) long

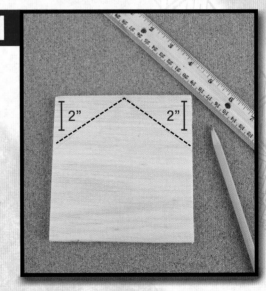

1

Measure and mark the center point of the front edge of the wood. Measure 2 inches (5 cm) down one side of the square and make a mark. Draw a line from this point to the center mark on the front edge. Repeat on the opposite side.

2

Ask an adult to help you cut along the lines with a hand saw to make the bow of the boat.

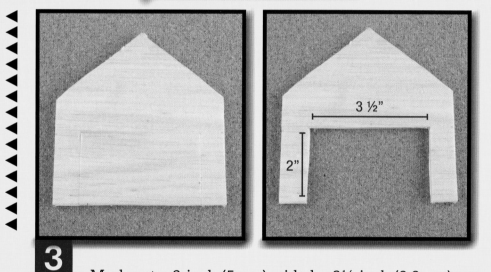

3

Mark out a 2-inch (5-cm) wide by 3½-inch (8.9-cm) long rectangle centered on the back side of the wood. Ask an adult to help you cut out this area of the wood.

3 ½"

2"

4

Trace the end of the soup can to draw two circles on the foam board. Ask an adult to help you cut out the circles with a utility knife. Use the nail to punch holes in the centers of the circles.

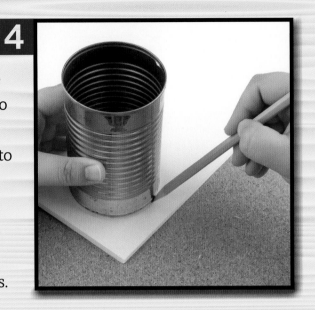

To make the paddle wheel for the boat, measure and mark the foam circles into fourths. Cut 1-inch (2.5-cm) slits at each mark on the outside edges. Slide the plastic strips from the milk jug into the slits of each circle. Glue the strips in place with hot glue.

5

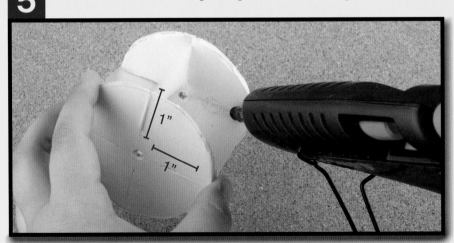

6

Insert the rubber band through the holes in the foam circles. Place the paddle wheel in the gap at the back of the wood. Hook the rubber band around the small ends. Glue the rubber band in place at the holes.

Use paint and stickers to decorate the boat. Wind the paddlewheel backward until the rubber band is tight. Place the boat in the water, let it go, and watch it cruise!

7

Formula One Race Car

If you're a race fan, here's a cool car for you. This awesome Formula One race car is simple, yet fast. Get ready to rev up this car's powerful rubber band engine!

✂ MATERIALS

- corrugated cardboard
- 2 wooden skewers
- 4 small washers
- 4 plastic potato chip can lids
- 1 large binder clip
- 1 large paper clip
- 3 large, thick rubber bands
- paint and paintbrush
- stickers

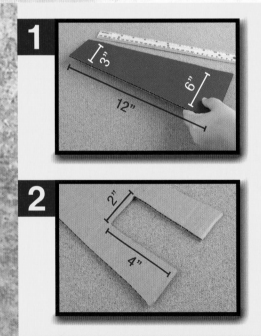

1

2

Draw and cut a trapezoid shape from the cardboard. It should be 12 inches (30 cm) long. Make one end 3 inches (7.6 cm) wide. Make the other end 6 inches (15 cm) wide. Be sure the holes inside the cardboard run sideways.

Cut out a notch 4 inches (10 cm) long by 2 inches (5 cm) wide on the wide end of the cardboard.

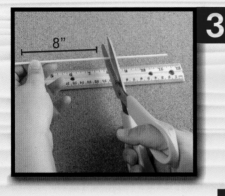

3

Measure and cut one skewer to 8 inches (20 cm) long. Cut the other skewer to 5½ inches (14 cm) long.

Poke a hole in the center of a plastic lid with a nail. Place the lid onto one end of the long skewer. Slide a washer over the skewer, then glue it in place onto the lid. Repeat this step with the short skewer.

4

5

Slide the long skewer through the cardboard about 1 inch (7.5 cm) from the wide end. Be sure it goes through the cut-out notch. Slide in the short skewer about 1 inch (7.5 cm) from the narrow end. Repeat step 4 to attach the other two lids on the other end of the skewers.

6

Spread open the paper clip slightly and clip it over the back axle. Wrap the paper clip with masking tape to secure it.

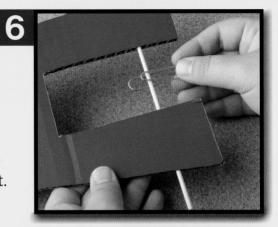

7

Wrap a rubber band around the outside of each back wheel to improve traction.

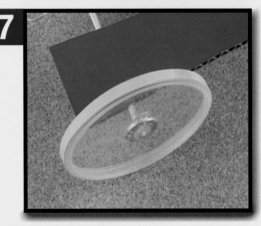

8

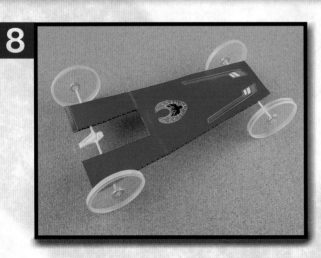

Paint and decorate the cardboard to make it look like a race car.

9

Place a rubber band inside the binder clip. Attach the binder clip to the inside of the notch.

Pull the rubber band back and catch it around the paper clip. Wind the clip backward several times. Place the car on the ground, release it, and watch it go!

10

TIP To strengthen the car, carefully fill the holes on the inside of the cardboard with white glue and let dry.

Water Blaster Rocket

Hot summer days are a time to get wet and wild. You'll have a blast watching this water rocket take off. Get ready to get soaked!

✂ MATERIALS

- ¼-inch (.64-cm) plastic tubing, 5 feet (1.5 m) long
- ¼-inch (.64-cm) copper tubing, 2 inches (5 cm) long
- #3 black rubber stopper with center hole
- 1 empty 2-liter soda bottle
- epoxy glue
- medium weight wire
- 1 bicycle valve stem
- bicycle pump
- piece of plywood about 5 inches (12.7 cm) wide by 16 inches (41 cm) long

1

Insert the copper tubing into the hole in the rubber stopper.

TIP Many of the materials for this project may be found at your local hardware store.

2

Insert the other end of the copper tubing into the plastic tubing.

3

Insert the other end of the plastic tubing into the bicycle valve stem.

4

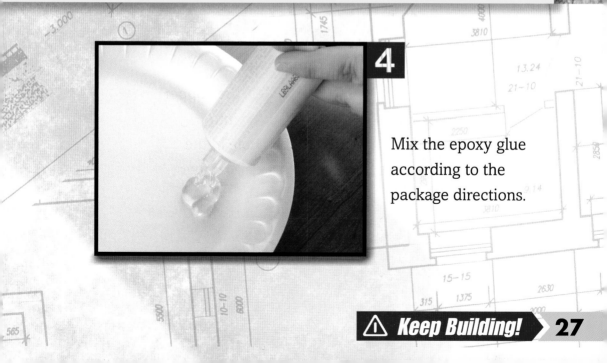

Mix the epoxy glue according to the package directions.

5

Use a toothpick to carefully spread the glue and seal all the connections from steps 1 to 3. Set the assembly aside to dry overnight.

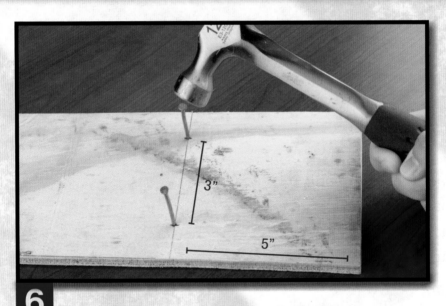

6

Measure and mark a line on the board 5 inches (12.7 cm) from the bottom. Pound in two nails about 3 inches (7.6 cm) apart on this line. Allow the nails to stick out about 1 inch (2.5 cm).

7 Measure and mark another line about 12 inches (30 cm) from the bottom of the board. Pound in two more nails about 5 inches (12.7 cm) apart.

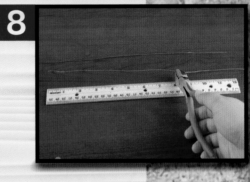

8 Measure and cut one piece of wire 12 inches (30 cm) long. Cut a second piece 8 inches (20 cm) long.

9 Place the 2-liter bottle on the board so it fits between the nails. Fit the top of the bottle into the narrower space. Wrap the wires around the heads of the nails to make loops that will hold the bottle. Be sure the wires are loose enough so the bottle can easily slide in and out.

10

When the glue is dry on the tubing assembly, fill the bottle about ⅓ full of water. Insert the rubber stopper tightly into the top of the bottle. Place the bottle in the launch pad.

11

Go outside to set up the launch pad. Prop it against a log, box, or concrete block so the rocket points upward.

12

Attach the bicycle pump to the valve stem.

Move several feet away from the launch pad and begin pumping the bicycle pump. The rocket will soon blast off while spraying you with water!

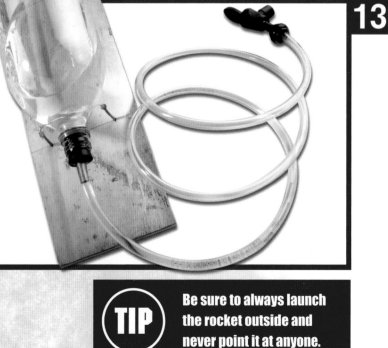

13

TIP Be sure to always launch the rocket outside and never point it at anyone.

Balmer, Alden J. *Doc Fizzix Mousetrap Racers: The Complete Builder's Manual.* East Petersburg, Pa.: Fox Chapel Pub., 2008.

Bell-Rehwoldt, Sheri. *The Kids' Guide to Building Cool Stuff.* Kids' Guides. Mankato, Minn.: Capstone Press, 2009.

Rigsby, Mike. *Amazing Rubber Band Cars: Easy-To-Build Wind-Up Racers, Models, and Toys.* Chicago: Chicago Review Press, 2008.

Internet Sites

FactHound offers a safe, fun way to find Internet sites related to this book. All of the sites on FactHound have been researched by our staff.

Here's all you do:

Visit *www.facthound.com*

Type in this code: 9781429654371

Super-cool stuff!

Check out projects, games and lots more at **www.capstonekids.com**